C I T Y !

NEW YORK

BY SHIRLEY CLIMO

PHOTOGRAPHS BY GEORGE ANCONA

MACMILLAN PUBLISHING COMPANY   NEW YORK

COLLIER MACMILLAN PUBLISHERS   LONDON

For Beverly R.,
with appreciation

—S.C.

To Cousin Richie and Iris

—G.A.

The author wishes to thank Dr. James Shenton,
Professor of History, Columbia University,
for his assistance in reviewing the factual content of this book.

Text copyright © 1990 by Shirley Climo · Photographs copyright © 1990 by George Ancona, except photograph 4A, page 4, by Isabel Ancona · Maps copyright © 1990 by Andrew Mudryk · All rights reserved. No part of this book may be reproduced or transmitted in any form or by any means, electronic or mechanical, including photocopying, recording, or by any information storage and retrieval system, without permission in writing from the Publisher. Macmillan Publishing Company, 866 Third Avenue, New York, NY 10022. Collier Macmillan Canada, Inc. First Edition Printed and bound in the United States of America 10   9   8   7   6   5   4   3   2   1

The text of this book is set in 12 point ITC Century Light. The photographs were taken on 35mm Kodachrome film and reproduced from color transparencies.
Library of Congress Cataloging-in-Publication Data · Climo, Shirley. City! New York / by Shirley Climo; photographs by George Ancona. — 1st ed.   p.   cm. Summary: Introduces the history, geography, cultural life, and attractions of the city known as the Big Apple. 1. New York (N.Y.)—Description—1981-   —Juvenile literature. 2. New York (N.Y.)—History—Juvenile literature. [1. New York (N.Y.)] I. Ancona, George, ill. II. Title. F128.33.C55 1990 974.7′1—dc20   89-13482 CIP AC   ISBN 0-02-719020-X

CONTENTS

ONE

Welcome to New York · 2

TWO

Going Dutch · 9

THREE

The Yankees Are Coming! · 15

FOUR

Growing Pains, Growing Pleasures · 20

FIVE

Ever Upward · 30

SIX

Exploring New York City · 42

SEVEN

A Pocketful of Facts · 53

Street Map of Manhattan · 56

Index · 58

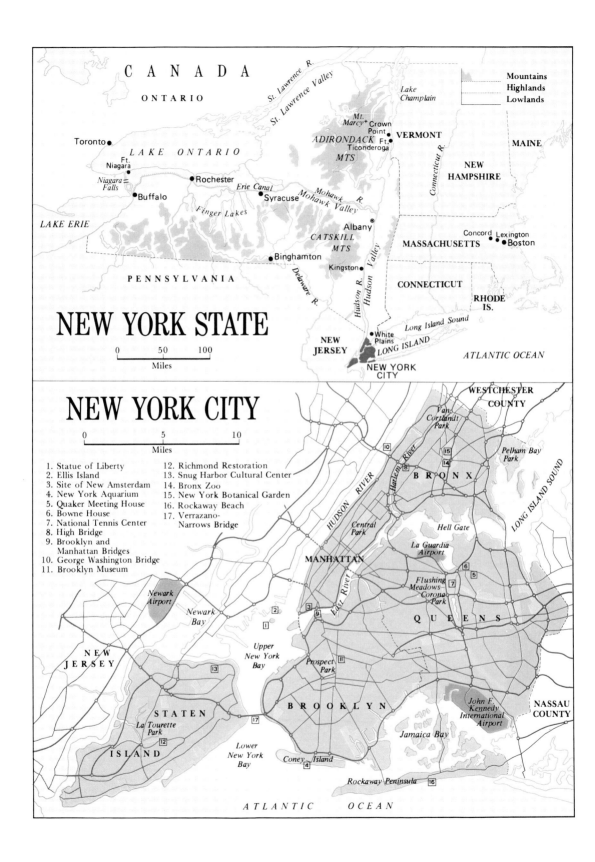

NEW YORK STATE

CANADA

ONTARIO

St. Lawrence R.
St. Lawrence Valley

Lake Champlain

Toronto

LAKE ONTARIO

Ft. Niagara

Niagara Falls

Buffalo

Rochester

Erie Canal

Syracuse

Finger Lakes

LAKE ERIE

Mt. Marcy

Crown Point

ADIRONDACK

Ft. Ticonderoga

MTS

VERMONT

MAINE

NEW HAMPSHIRE

Connecticut R.

Mohawk R.

Mohawk Valley

Albany

CATSKILL MTS

Binghamton

Kingston

Hudson R.

Hudson Valley

Delaware R.

PENNSYLVANIA

Concord Lexington
Boston

MASSACHUSETTS

CONNECTICUT

RHODE IS.

White Plains

Long Island Sound

LONG ISLAND

ATLANTIC OCEAN

NEW JERSEY

NEW YORK CITY

Mountains
Highlands
Lowlands

0	50	100

Miles

NEW YORK CITY

0	5	10

Miles

1. Statue of Liberty
2. Ellis Island
3. Site of New Amsterdam
4. New York Aquarium
5. Quaker Meeting House
6. Bowne House
7. National Tennis Center
8. High Bridge
9. Brooklyn and Manhattan Bridges
10. George Washington Bridge
11. Brooklyn Museum

12. Richmond Restoration
13. Snug Harbor Cultural Center
14. Bronx Zoo
15. New York Botanical Garden
16. Rockaway Beach
17. Verrazano-Narrows Bridge

WESTCHESTER COUNTY

Van Cortlandt Park

Pelham Bay Park

HUDSON RIVER

Harlem River

BRONX

LONG ISLAND SOUND

Central Park

Hell Gate

La Guardia Airport

MANHATTAN

East River

Flushing Meadows Corona Park

QUEENS

Newark Airport

Newark Bay

NEW JERSEY

Upper New York Bay

Prospect Park

BROOKLYN

John F. Kennedy International Airport

NASSAU COUNTY

STATEN

La Tourette Park

ISLAND

Lower New York Bay

Coney Island

Jamaica Bay

Rockaway Peninsula

ATLANTIC OCEAN

A.▲ B.▼ C.▼

A. Sightseers enjoy a view of lower Manhattan. B. Some visitors choose to cruise around the entire island. C. Cart-wheeling vendors have sold snacks on New York City streets for three hundred years.

O N E

WELCOME TO NEW YORK

Once there was a town named New Orange. It grew up to be a city nicknamed the Big Apple. How that orange became an apple is part of the story of America's biggest, most exciting city. And that's New York, New York.

Both the city and the state share the same name. New York City is at the southeastern tip of New York State, where the Hudson River meets the Atlantic Ocean.

New York City is many cities in one. Within its boundaries are five separate sections, called boroughs. Each borough manages its own local affairs. But, since each is also part of the greater city of New York, the citizens of the five boroughs elect a single mayor.

Queens is by far the largest of the boroughs, measuring over one hundred square miles. The borough of Brooklyn, covering close to eighty square miles, is next in size. Look for both Queens and Brooklyn on Long Island.

Smaller Staten Island, almost sixty-one square miles, is in New York Bay. On a map, it looks as if Staten Island should belong to the nearby state of New Jersey. But, long ago, New York State won the island in a contest. In 1668, before the two were even states, New York and New Jersey agreed that any island that could be sailed around in twenty-four hours would belong to New York. Captain Christopher Billopp raced his boat around Staten Island in just twenty-three hours!

Although only forty-three miles square, the Bronx occupies a special place. It is on the mainland. The Bronx is the only New York City borough that's part of the continental United States.

Manhattan is the smallest of the five boroughs. Manhattan Island is shaped somewhat like an Indian moccasin, just over thirteen miles long and less than two-and-a-half miles across at its widest point. It looks quite different from most islands seen in travel advertisements. Manhattan sprouts skyscrapers instead of palm trees, and the tall buildings hide the surrounding water from view. But Manhattan is a genuine island, just the same. The Hudson River flows along the west side of the island, and the East River along the east. The Harlem River edges Manhattan on the north, and New York Bay lies at its southern tip.

For hundreds of years, when people spoke of New York City they meant Manhattan. It was the original New York, and it is still the part of the city that everyone wants most to visit. Manhattan skyscrapers are pictured on postcards, and the streets of Manhattan are the settings for many songs and stories and movies. In fact, the earliest movies were made in Manhattan, not Hollywood.

A.▲   B.▼

A. Rockefeller Center heralds the coming of Christmas. B. Holiday scenes brighten winter windows in Fifth Avenue stores.

OPPOSITE PAGE: A. Spring arrives in the Sculpture Garden of the Museum of Modern Art. B. Summer is the season for relaxing in the Sheep Meadow in Central Park. C. In autumn, Central Park is a celebration of color.

.A.▲ B.▲ C.▼

All together, the five boroughs cover a huge area. But you can't measure New York by miles alone. It's the people who count—if you can count them! Over seven million people call New York home, making it the largest city in the United States.

Anytime you can come to New York is a wonderful time to visit. In winter, Manhattan's smoky gray buildings are dusted with snow, like powdered sugar. Even the traffic lights wear white caps. At holiday season, giant man-made snowflakes turn Fifth Avenue into a blizzard of lights. Skaters skim across the ice at Central Park's Wollman Rink, and hot roasted chestnuts are for sale on street corners. But be sure to bring your muffler and mittens, for the average temperature in January is thirty-two degrees Fahrenheit.

Travel lightly in the summer. The city can be as hot and steamy as a sauna, so change into your shorts and sandals. Of course there are lots of air-conditioned shops and restaurants, but it's more fun to catch the breeze aboard a boat. The Staten Island ferry runs between Staten Island and Manhattan.

Spring and fall are the pick of the seasons. In March or April Rockefeller Center is decked out in tulips and daffodils for the Easter Parade. In the clear, crisp days of autumn, the trees in Central Park blaze with red and orange leaves. But be prepared for surprises. Springtime showers can turn to hail, and Jack Frost sometimes arrives, uninvited, in the middle of Indian summer. Even though New York City has had a weather observatory for 165 years—the first station in the nation—New Yorkers can only do what everyone else does about the weather: talk about it.

Trains enter Manhattan through underground tunnels. If you come by rail, you won't know you're in New York until you hear the conductor call, "Grand Central Terminal!" or perhaps, "Next stop, Penn-syl-va-ni-a Station!"

If you arrive by airplane, your first sight of the city will be of Queens. John F. Kennedy and La Guardia airports are located in that borough. By day, you'll look down on a sand-colored landscape of concrete buildings and a maze of road-ways. You'll see the silvery shine of the waterways, as well, and the bridges that span them. Like ribbons, these bridges tie the boroughs together. By night, millions of yellow lights flicker far below, broken only by the darker streaks that are the rivers and the midnight blackness beyond that is the Atlantic Ocean.

New York is America's Atlantic gateway. If your parents, or your grandparents, or your great-grandparents came from Europe, a breathtaking skyline greeted them. Seen from a ship sailing into the bay, Manhattan rises up from the water like a city in a pop-up storybook. The Statue of Liberty stands in the harbor. Torch upraised, she has saluted newcomers for more than a century. Her message is the same in any language:

¡Bienvenida! Willkomen! Benvenuto! Shalom! Yō Koso!

Welcome to New York!

A. The Statue of Liberty, towering three hundred feet above the waterline, is visible from ship or shore. B. "I lift my lamp beside the golden door." (From the poem by Emma Lazarus, which appears on the statue's base.)

A. ▲   B. ▼

T W O
←——————→
GOING
DUTCH

Sixteen million people visit New York City each year. But a few men came before the crowd, even before there was a city to visit at all.

The first European arrived in New York Bay in 1524. His name was Giovanni da Verrazano, and he was an Italian explorer hired by the king of France. Verrazano was searching for the Northwest Passage, a legendary waterway across North America to Asia. Although he sailed into what is New York's harbor today, he did not linger. A gale was blowing up, so Verrazano returned to the deeper, safer waters of the sea.

Later that year, a second visitor drifted in. His name was Estéban Gómez, and he was a black navigator seeking treasure for the king of Spain. The hills of New York on a gray winter day did not show much golden promise. Gómez decided that going ashore would be a waste of time.

Eighty-five years passed before another European adventurer came to call. Henry Hudson, an Englishman, was exploring for a company, not a king. Hudson had been hired by the Dutch East India Company to try to find that hoped-for Northwest Passage. Captain Hudson steered his small ship, the *Half Moon*, up the river that now bears his name. He did not discover a shortcut to Asia, but he did find curious and friendly Indians camped on an island at the river's mouth. The Algonquin Indians called this place *Manhattan*, "island of the hills." Henry Hudson stayed for a full month, swapping cookpots and trinkets with the Indians for beaver and otter skins. He wrote in his log: "It is as pleasant a land as one can tread upon."

In that same year, 1609, another unexpected guest appeared, but from a different direction. The French explorer Samuel de Champlain crossed into what is present-day New York State from Canada. He claimed this new territory for France, a claim that would lead to trouble nearly a century later.

Thanks to Hudson's explorations, the Dutch East India Company took possession of all the land between the English colony of Virginia to the south and the English colonies of New England to the north. The company named its province New Netherland, and set up a Dutch West India Company to manage its affairs.

In 1624, the Dutch West India Company paid the passage for eight families to come to Manhattan Island. They called their community New Amsterdam. The next year, four more boatloads of settlers—and dozens of cows and pigs and horses—joined them. The company appointed a director general to live in the colony and oversee its business.

The colony's business was beavers. Thousands of beaver

skins were sent back to Holland to be made into warm felt hats. Manhattan Island was a favorite Indian hunting ground, for it was home not only to beavers and otters, but also to bears, wolves, foxes, and even mountain lions! Most tribes were eager to trade fur for strings of shiny oblong beads called *wampum*, or for sturdy woolen duffel cloth woven in Holland.

But the Dutch were uneasy about sharing the island with their Indian neighbors. In the early summer of 1626, Peter Minuit, the director general, bought Manhattan from them for beads and cloth and fishhooks worth about twenty-four dollars. Today Manhattan's price tag would be more than sixty *billion* dollars, but both Dutch and Indians thought they had made a splendid bargain.

English, Irish, German, French, Danish, Swedish, and African settlers joined the Dutch in New Amsterdam. By 1643, eighteen different languages were spoken on the streets of New Amsterdam. Besides the trappers and traders who worked for the company, the townspeople included blacksmiths and bakers, woodcutters and chimney sweeps, soldiers and slaves. Protestants, Catholics, and Quakers practiced their religions, and, within a few years, the first Jews had arrived from Brazil.

Still, New Amsterdam looked definitely Dutch. Like those in Holland, some houses were faced with red or yellow brick and topped with tile roofs. By 1642, Manhattan even had its first skyscraper—a long-armed Dutch windmill!

A. Dutch traders and American Indians greeted one another with curiosity and caution (Museum of the City of New York). B, C. On the Surrogates Court building, an Indian and a Dutchman stand as reminders of New York's beginnings. D. A plaque on the base of the Battery Park flagpole marks the founding of New York City. E. Peter Stuyvesant welcomes an Algonquin Indian (American Museum of Natural History).

A. ▲

ON THE
____ OF APRIL 1625 THE
AMSTERDAM CHAMBER OF
THE WEST INDIA COMPANY
DECREED THE ESTABLISHMENT
OF FORT AMSTERDAM
AND THE CREATION OF
THE ADJOINING FARMS
THE PURCHASE OF THE
ISLAND OF MANHATTAN
WAS ACCOMPLISHED IN
1626 THUS WAS LAID THE
FOUNDATION OF THE
CITY OF NEW YORK

B. ▲   C. ▲   D. ▲   E. ▼

Progress and problems went hand in hand in the colony. The citizens of New Amsterdam were worried by the growing English settlements on Long Island and by the increasing number of Swedish landowners moving into Delaware. Moreover, hostile Indians made repeated raids on New Amsterdam. In 1644, to protect the city from enemies, Director Willem Kieft ordered "a good stiff fence" twelve feet high built on the north side of town. The wooden wall ran across the entire island, and the path beside it was called "Waal," or Wall, Street. Although the wall is long gone, today's Wall Street follows that original lane.

The last Dutch director general was Petrus—or Peter—Stuyvesant. He was the original "Peg-Leg Pete," for he had lost a leg in battle and wore a wooden peg, trimmed in silver. From the time Director Stuyvesant arrived in 1647, he ruled New Amsterdam with strict laws, a sharp tongue, and an iron fist. He was the *boss*, a word that comes from the Dutch *baas*, meaning "master."

To discourage pigs from roaming, Stuyvesant declared that anyone caught throwing garbage into the streets must pay a fine. This was America's first litter law—and to help to enforce it and other decrees, Peter Stuyvesant ordered the construction of a stout jail.

In 1658, Director Stuyvesant started the first paid police force in the country. Nicknamed the Prowlers, they patrolled the city at night, on the lookout for lawbreakers. They worried more about fire than about crime, and if a

Prowler saw a blaze beginning, he clattered a huge wooden rattle to awaken the volunteer fire brigade.

Even under Stuyvesant's vigilant eye, the troubles of the Dutch West India Company grew worse. The English were squeezing New Amsterdam from every direction. In 1664, Charles II, the king of England, gave his brother James, the Duke of York, all of Long Island and the city of New Amsterdam as a present. At once the Duke of York sent four gunboats into the harbor.

Stuyvesant was furious and tried to rally the citizens of New Amsterdam. But the practical townspeople refused to fight. Without a shot being fired, the city surrendered. The orange and white and blue banner of the Dutch West India Company was hauled down, and the red, white, and blue flag of England was raised above the city walls.

The Duke of York promptly renamed New Netherland and New Amsterdam. He called them both New York. But, nine years later, his pride took a tumble. Britain and the Netherlands went to war. This time it was the Dutch who sailed their warships into the harbor. The Dutch retook New York City.

The city then became New Orange, after the Dutch prince William of Orange—but not for long. When the war ended in 1674, New Orange was returned to England as part of the peace treaty.

The name New Orange was changed back to New York. And New York City it has remained.

THREE

←——→

THE YANKEES
ARE COMING!

Janke is a Dutch nickname for Jan, or John. English soldiers scornfully called any Dutchman a "Janke," pronounced yahn-key. Over the years, the spelling became Yankee. And, over the years, a different kind of Yankee came along.

Under English rule, New York remained a trading town. Schooners and sloops sailed from the harbor loaded with lumber, furs, and tobacco, bound for European ports. They returned with holds crammed with manufactured goods and with new immigrants. As the city grew, so did its mix of peoples.

New York became known for fashion. Young dandies, called *fribbles*, wore curled and powdered wigs and fastened their velvet breeches at the knee with silver buckles. Women paraded through the cobblestone streets in skirts like sails, buoyed up with petticoats.

But there were New Yorkers dressed in rags, as well, for most land was still held by the wealthy in large estates. Citizens grumbled, and slaves revolted. In 1741, two thousand of the population of ten thousand were African slaves.

The English faced problems on both sides of the Atlantic Ocean. In 1689, war broke out between England and France.

A.▲   B.►

A. Five historic sailing ships are anchored at the South Street Seaport. B. George Washington watches passersby from the steps of Federal Hall National Memorial, the site where he became the first president of the United States.

The two countries fought not only in Europe but also in North America. Most of the fighting on this continent took place in Canada, but there were battles in New York State, as well, over France's claim to the land explored by Samuel de Champlain earlier in the century. These struggles dragged on for seventy-four years, and, in this country, they were known as the French and Indian Wars. The Algonquin Indians helped the French, and the Iroquois Indians sided with the English. Among the bloody battlefields in New York State were Fort Niagara, Fort Ticonderoga, and Crown Point.

In 1763, England and France signed the Treaty of Paris, and France gave up most of her North American possessions. But an end to the fighting did not bring an end to American troubles. George III had become king of England, and many of his actions angered his American subjects.

In 1765, King George put a tax on all documents, even newspapers. Called the Stamp Act, it was intended to raise money to keep British troops in the colonies. The colonists

A.◄ B.▲

A. After the Revolutionary War, General Washington said good-bye to his officers at Fraunces Tavern. B. Dolls display costumes of the American past in the Museum of the City of New York.

thought the tax was unfair, and they didn't want to support any English soldiers. They decided to boycott British goods until the tax was removed. Groups of patriots called the Sons of Liberty were organized. In New York, the fribbles gave up fancy clothes and took up the slogan, "Better to wear a homespun coat than lose our liberty!"

The Stamp Act was repealed, but King George wanted to teach the disobedient colonists a lesson. He placed new taxes on paper, glass, lead, and tea. In a protest similar to the Boston Tea Party, New Yorkers dumped the cargo from a British tea ship into the Hudson River.

On April 23, 1775, New York City heard startling news: Four days earlier, British troops and American Minutemen—volunteers ready and willing to answer a call to arms—had met in actual battle near two small Massachusetts towns, Concord and Lexington. The American Revolution had begun.

American colonists chose George Washington as their commander in chief. General Washington, who had served as a major in the French and Indian Wars, drove the British from Massachusetts. On April 4, 1776, he arrived in New York to defend that city.

New York was now the third largest city in the colonies, after Philadelphia and Boston. About half of the twenty-five thousand New Yorkers were patriots, but the other half were Tories, or Loyalists—those loyal to the English king.

General Washington's Continental Army was a disarray of farmers and tradesmen, grandfathers and schoolboys. The British and the Tories laughed at these Yankee rebels as they had at the Dutch *Jankes*.

On August 27, 1776, British and American soldiers clashed in the Battle of Long Island. The thirty-two thousand British troops outnumbered Washington's army two to one, and the Americans scattered in retreat. Had it not been for the cover of fog and rain, George Washington himself might have been captured.

Washington's forces withdrew across the East River into Manhattan, and, in September, the British and the Americans fought again at the Battle of Harlem Heights. This time the Continental Army proved its fighting power. But General Washington knew his small army could not hold New York City, and he retreated to a place called White Plains.

In all, ninety-two battles were fought in New York State. But in that late summer of 1776, New York City fell into British hands, and there it remained until the war's end.

New York became a refuge for Tories from all over the

colonies. Soon after the American forces pulled out, the city caught fire. Some blamed the Tories. Others said that retreating rebels had set the blaze. Whatever the cause, the fire was soon out of control. When it had finally burned itself out, one thousand buildings were in ashes, and one-third of the city had been destroyed. Crammed with British soldiers, their families, and Loyalists, New York was impossibly overcrowded. So many canvas tents were hastily thrown up that the city was called Canvas Town.

In October 1781, British General Charles Cornwallis surrendered to George Washington at Yorktown, Virginia. While the drums kept the beat, the fife played "Yankee Doodle." American Yankees had come to stay.

November 25, 1783, was Evacuation Day, a date that for decades New Yorkers celebrated like the Fourth of July. This was the day that English troops evacuated the city, and General Washington's victorious Continental Army returned.

When the United States Congress met on January 11, 1785, it chose New York City as its first capital. In July 1788, the New York legislature ratified the Constitution and became the country's eleventh state.

But New York City's greatest day was yet to come. On April 30, 1789, George Washington stood on the balcony of the Federal Building on Broad Street. Dressed in a plain brown suit of homespun cloth, he proudly took the oath that made him the first president of the United States.

FOUR

GROWING PAINS, GROWING PLEASURES

New York City was the nation's capital for only one year. Then the government moved its headquarters to Philadelphia.

On April 30, 1790, George Washington left New York, never to return again. But Washington had confidence in the future of both the city and state of New York. In 1783, he had predicted that the state might become "the seat of a new empire." George Washington's words inspired New York's nickname, the Empire State.

In the census of 1800, New York City counted more than sixty thousand people. Within a few years, it would be the biggest city in the country. Already it was the busiest. The rivers were clogged with boats, and the wooden masts of ships in the harbor were as thick as trees in a forest. In 1807, New Yorkers stared in astonishment at a strange new vessel with a smokestack instead of a mast. Robert Fulton's steamboat puffed and snorted its way up the Hudson River at a breathtaking four miles an hour!

A.▲ B.▲ C.▼

A., B. Traffic jams the streets and sidewalks of America's biggest and busiest city.
C. Now tall buildings rise above Battery Park, but once a group of guns, called a *battery,* guarded the harbor. That's how the park got its name.

Day and night, carts and carriages rumbled through the streets of New York City. Traffic jammed the crooked lanes, and the hodgepodge of houses was confusing. In 1811, John Randel, a surveyor, proposed a street system for the remaining open lands of Manhattan Island. Streets running from east to west would be straight, and numbered in order. Avenues, also numbered, were to go from north to south. Blocks would be laid out in neat rectangles. Even today, with more than six thousand miles of streets, it's easier to find your way in Manhattan than in any other large city.

Putting Randel's plan into action meant blasting granite cliffs, leveling hills, tearing out trees, and draining grassy marshlands. If they had foreseen Manhattan's future, the Indians never would have called it "island of hills." The island also has grown far larger than their old hunting ground. All of New York's waterfront is built on *landfill*, land that was created by dumping thousands of tons of earth and stones into the water.

The United States and Britain went to war again in 1812. New York State furnished both men and supplies for the war effort, but New York City wasn't the scene of any battles. At the end of the war in 1814, New York State had the greatest population in the nation. Its new governor, De Witt Clinton, had a dream for the state big enough to match its size. He planned a canal between Albany and Buffalo, a city on Lake Erie. Then ships could sail up the Hudson River and into the Great Lakes.

When work began, New Yorkers chuckled and called the canal Clinton's Ditch or Clinton's Coffin. But no one laughed when the Erie Canal was finished in 1825. It was the longest canal in the world, 363 miles, and opened the American West to trade and settlers. Now New York was the nation's chief port for domestic as well as foreign commerce.

December 16, 1835, was the day of the Great Fire. Flames raced along Broad Street, Wall Street, and through the East River area. Although New York City had installed the first fire hydrants in 1808, the weather was so cold that the water had frozen. The firefighters, manning their hand-pump engines, could do little to keep the area that had once been New Amsterdam from burning. When the cinders had cooled, New York rebuilt, but the old part of the city was gone forever.

By the middle of the nineteenth century, floods of im-migrants had begun to pour into New York City. Primarily from northern Europe, three million arrived in the sixteen years between 1840 and 1856. The huge numbers over-whelmed New Yorkers. Even the residents who had been newcomers themselves a few years before were hostile to later arrivals. They feared for their jobs and even their lives, for they blamed any outbreaks of disease on the new im-migrants. The Irish, who had fled the potato famine in Ire-land, outnumbered immigrants from all other countries put together, so they were particular targets of prejudice.

There was such a shortage of housing that many had to

crowd into cellars or backyard shanties. Lack of work pushed gangs of men, such as the Bowery Boys, into the streets. The police, not a uniformed force until 1853, could neither keep peace nor protect property.

The worst troubles came during the Civil War. New York State supplied more men and materials for the Union cause than did any other northern state. But the citizens of New York City were divided in their loyalties. Most did not support slavery, for slaves within the city had been freed more than thirty years before, on July 4, 1827. But many did not support the war, either. Some thought it was bad for business. Others resented the draft to raise the Union army. A man with means might buy out of the draft by giving the government three hundred dollars. Few immigrants could afford that kind of money. They called the Civil War "a rich man's war but a poor man's fight." The Draft Riots of 1863 lasted for four days and tore New York City apart. No one knows the number killed, but some say as many Americans died in the New York riots as had lost their lives in the War of 1812.

Still, for each new rush of foreigners that pressed down the gangplanks, New York was a place of golden promise. For some, that promise came true.

Lower Fifth Avenue became the stylish address. Elegant mansions lined the streets, and a new word was coined for the very rich: *millionaire*. John Jacob Astor had arrived as an immigrant in 1783, but when he died in 1848, he was

A. ◄ B. ▼

C. ▼ D. ▼

A, B. The New York City Fire Department Museum recalls past years, when the "fire laddies" were New York's heroes. C. The triangular Flatiron Building is so called because it resembles an old-fashioned pressing iron. D. Once the Astor library, this enormous old building now houses the Public Theater.

the richest man in America. The Astor family reigned over New York society for generations.

By day, New York was a bustling business and shopping center. Broadway had become such a snarl of carriages, delivery wagons, and horse-drawn omnibuses that it might take a pedestrian half an hour to cross the street!

At night, New York glittered beneath the gaslights. There were costume balls, theater, concerts, and opera to attend.

An outdoor attraction brought the most pleasure to the most people. In 1858, designs were drawn for a huge city park. When it was finished a dozen years later, swampland had been turned into two-and-a-half miles of hills and trees, ponds and paths. Central Park brought the country back to Manhattan.

In 1853, the city held its first world's fair. In that same year, the Women's Rights Convention met, and Miss Lucy Stone shocked the city by appearing in bloomers.

In 1859, Otis Tufts installed in a Fifth Avenue hotel the world's first elevator. He called it a "vertical railway."

In 1874, the American Museum of Natural History opened. Also that year, ground was broken for the permanent home of the Metropolitan Museum of Art.

In 1879, telephones came to the city. Operators began conversations by shouting, "Ahoy!" into the mouthpiece. That same year, the famous stone and marble Saint Patrick's Cathedral was dedicated. It had taken twenty years to build.

In 1882, Thomas A. Edison electrified Manhattan with

his "incandescent lamp." Twenty-five years later, one hundred thousand bulbs would light three thousand signs in New York City.

May 24, 1883, looked like the Fourth of July in New York. Fireworks celebrated the opening of the Brooklyn Bridge between Manhattan and Brooklyn. Its towers—329 feet high—were the tallest structures in New York. The Brooklyn Bridge was declared a National Historic Monument in 1964.

On a rainy Thursday in October 1886, the Statue of Liberty was dedicated. Its creator was a sculptor named Frédéric A. Bartholdi, and the statue was a gift from the people of France to the people of the United States. American school children collected nickels and dimes to help pay for its base. The goddess Liberty stands 151 feet tall and has a thirty-five-foot waistline. Even her fingernails measure more than a foot across!

Good times did not mean good government for New York. The city spent these years of progress under the control of a crooked political organization called Tammany Hall. The worst of the dishonest politicians was William Marcy— "Boss"—Tweed. Tammany Hall did make one timely contribution. On June 1, 1898, Manhattan, Brooklyn, the Bronx, Queens, and Richmond (now Staten Island) were merged, and Greater New York City was born. The combined boroughs had more than three and a half million people. In all the world, only London was larger. Not even George Washington imagined such a tremendous city.

A. Central Park is an island of green in midtown Manhattan. B., C. The Bethesda Fountain and the Alice in Wonderland sculpture are favorite park attractions.
D., E. The Temple of Dendur from ancient Egypt is among the thousands of exhibits at the huge Metropolitan Museum of Art.

B.▲ C.▼

A.▲

D.▼ E.►

A. President and naturalist Theodore Roosevelt welcomes you to the American Museum of Natural History. B., C. Inside the museum, which contains forty halls, visitors can gawk at dinosaurs and elephants. D. In the adjoining Hayden Planetarium, they can gaze at stars. E. Saint Patrick's Cathedral has been a Fifth Avenue landmark for over a century.

A. ◄   B. ▲

E. ▼

C. ▲   D. ▼

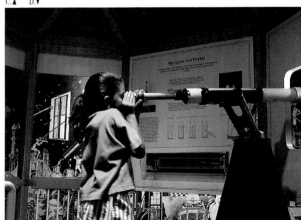

EVER UPWARD

The motto for the state of New York is "Ever upward!" Those two words are even more fitting for the city.

Early in this century, a mountain range of skyscrapers began to thrust above the streets of Manhattan. The island's base of hard granite could support the heaviest weight. The steel skeletons of the tall, thin structures, although appearing as fragile as spiderwebs, proved tough enough to withstand the strongest winds. And those amazing elevators easily whisked passengers to the topmost floors. Like a staircase, New York City's buildings climbed up story by story, year by year.

In 1902, the Flatiron Building was constructed. Triangular in shape and twenty-one stories high, it was the tallest building in town. Eleven years later, New Yorkers craned their necks to stare at Frank W. Woolworth's sixty-story skyscraper. The Woolworth Building cost the five-and-ten-cent-store king a lot of nickels and dimes: $13,500,000! When United States President Woodrow Wilson pushed the button that turned on the building's eighty thousand lights, people as far away as New Jersey blinked.

In 1930, the gleaming metallic needle on top of the

seventy-seven-story Chrysler Building spiked the sky. Two years later, the Empire State Building was finished. Its 102 stories made the skyscraper the world's tallest. A minute's ear-popping ride in the elevator takes visitors to the observatory on the 86 floor or to the smaller, glassed-in deck on the 102. But, beware! If the elevator's out of order, it's 1,860 steps to the bottom.

Since 1973, the two towers of the World Trade Center, each 110 stories high, have dominated the Manhattan skyline. Looking like side-by-side Cracker Jack boxes, the towers are cities in themselves. Fifty thousand people work there, and twice that number visit daily. Each tower is so large that it has its own zip code.

By the twentieth century, Manhattan's transportation troubles had gone from bad to terrible. Hundreds of thousands of people tried to squeeze onto the horse-drawn tram cars each day. To relieve the overcrowded streets, an elevated railway was built. The clatter of the "El" trains overhead frightened the horses. Soot and hot cinders dropped to the sidewalks below, and smoke poured into second-story windows. Since building up only added to the problems, the city decided to burrow down, instead. In 1900, twelve thousand workers began digging beneath Manhattan streets. And in 1904, the first nine miles of subway track was completed. Now subway trains travel along more than two hundred miles of track under New York City and carry more passengers than any other railway in the world.

A. ▲ B. ▲   C. ▲ D. ▼

A.▲ B.▲ C.▼ D.▼

OPPOSITE PAGE: A., B., C. Three of Manhattan's most famous skyscrapers are the Empire State Building, the Chrysler Building, and the Twin Towers of the World Trade Center. D. The view is breathtaking from the Observation Deck of the Empire State Building.

THIS PAGE: A. Horse-drawn carriages are still for hire, but now they're used only for fun. B., C. Also fun is taking a drive across the Brooklyn Bridge or the Verrazano-Narrows Bridge. D. But most New Yorkers get from here to there—or anywhere—by subway.

Some of the subways run through tubes under the rivers. In 1904, sixteen men strolled from New Jersey to Manhattan in a tunnel beneath the Hudson. People predicted that the tunnel would collapse from the weight of the water, but now twenty-two such tubes carry traffic underneath the city's rivers.

By 1917, motor vehicles outnumbered horses on the streets of Manhattan. Bigger and better bridges were needed for automobiles. The George Washington Bridge was built across the Hudson in 1931. Besides the Brooklyn Bridge, eight other bridges now cross the East River. The extensive Triborough Bridge system links the Bronx, Queens, and Manhattan. One of the newest is the Verrazano-Narrows Bridge, opened in 1964. One of the oldest is the High Bridge. Travelers have taken it across the Harlem River for almost 150 years.

Immigrants continued to stream into New York. By the turn of the century, Italians, Russians, Poles, Greeks, and others from central and southern Europe were in the majority. Many of these were Jews fleeing oppression.

Ellis Island, in New York Bay, was converted from a fort to an immigration reception center in 1891. Although intended to screen poorer immigrants for disease, the center often held healthy new arrivals for weeks. The center was officially closed in 1954, and, eleven years later, President Lyndon B. Johnson made Ellis Island a national monument. Almost half of all Americans alive today have ancestors who first stepped onto United States soil at Ellis Island.

Newcomers usually settled among people of their own background. There are Irish neighborhoods, Jewish neighborhoods, and many others, including Little Italy, Little India, and Chinatown. African-Americans from our own south moved to New York's Harlem on the west side, and Puerto Ricans and Cubans created Spanish Harlem on the east side of Manhattan. More than seventy-five languages are spoken in New York. You can take a trip around the world without ever leaving the city.

People of like interests also grouped together. Greenwich Village, once home to poets and painters, is one of the city's oldest sections.

During World War I, instead of welcoming ships packed with immigrants, New Yorkers waved good-bye to United States troops sailing to Europe. New York was the port for the American Expeditionary Forces, headed for battlefields in France. When the war ended in 1918, soldiers paraded up Fifth Avenue beneath a blizzard of ticker tape and torn paper.

Wall Street, headquarters for the New York Stock Exchange, had been the nation's business capital. World War I made it the world's financial center.

Fifth Avenue became the street for fashion in the 1920s, with small specialty shops and huge department stores. Park Avenue became the smart address for residences. Besides private houses, apartments also came into style.

A.▲ B.▼   C.▲ D.▼

A. In New York's Diamond District, two Orthodox Jews stop to talk. B. *Gelato* (Italian ice cream) is a treat found in Little Italy. C., D. Residents shop in Chinatown, and hungry visitors master chopsticks there.

A. The Apollo Theatre in Harlem is a showcase for African-American entertainers. B. Spanish is spoken in the streets of East Harlem. C. The marble arch in Washington Square Park is the symbol of Greenwich Village. D. An African vendor in midtown checks his wares.

Theaters are a New York tradition. George Washington and Abraham Lincoln both went to the theater here. In 1927, there were 268 shows on Broadway! Theater marquees, blazing with electric lights, gave Broadway the name the Great White Way. Top plays are still billed as Broadway hits, although now only one theater is located there.

In the twenties, Americans everywhere began to tap toes to jazz. Jazz musicians were the first to call New York the Big Apple. "There are a lot of apples dangling on the tree," they said, "but there's only one Big Apple." They meant that New York City was really the top.

The stock market crashed on Wall Street in October 1929. The world was caught in the Great Depression. For New York, the carnival days of the twenties were finished. One out of every four workers in the city of New York was unemployed. The jobless sold pencils and apples on the avenues. The homeless camped in tents in Central Park.

In the middle of the Depression, in 1932, Fiorello La Guardia was elected mayor of New York City. Only five feet tall, he was nicknamed the Little Flower. La Guardia began public housing systems and added more than five thousand acres to the city's parks. Most important, he ended the corrupt control by Tammany Hall on New York politics.

World War II broke out in 1941. Again, American troops sailed from New York Harbor to Europe, this time to fight the Axis powers of Germany and Italy. Until the war's end in 1945, the city's lights were dimmed in brownouts nightly so that ships at sea would not be illuminated. There were also practice blackouts, when not even a flashlight shone.

New York is called "the city that's never finished." Day and night, there are workers in the streets, above the streets, and under the streets. As if to music, the city marches to the rattle and the rumble of machines.

Unfortunately, trouble is another tune to which New York dances. In recent years, crime, strikes, and racial conflicts have been repeated themes. The clamor for more housing is heard, as well, especially from those people whose only homes are city streets and parks.

Most large American cities share these same concerns. But because New York is the largest, so are its difficulties.

Turmoil in the city is often featured on the national news. But New York has good news to broadcast, too. It is still America's business leader, and the capital for culture and entertainment. More important events take place in this city than any place else in the world. To send that message, New York reached into the past for a symbol: the Big Apple. No longer just musicians' slang, you'll hear it everywhere. And you'll see an apple on souvenirs from bumper stickers to gold jewelry. New York City *is* the Big Apple.

A., B. Manhattan is famous for its theater. Even the early Dutch watched plays here. C. Manhattan is also famous for its Stock Exchange, the marketplace for American business. D. The city is first in fashion.

OPPOSITE PAGE: A. And it's first in fancy stores. B., C. Two of Manhattan's other trademarks are building and rebuilding. The Cathedral of St. John the Divine has been under construction for a century, and the Fifth Avenue Presbyterian Church is now being renovated.

A.▼   B.►

C.▼   D.▼

A.▲ B.▼ C.▼

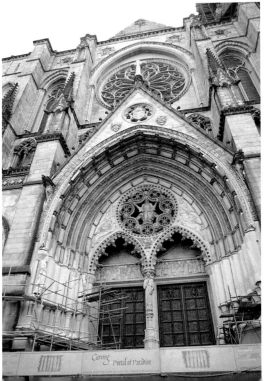

SIX

←——————————————→

EXPLORING
NEW YORK CITY

You can explore New York City just by standing still.

In the daytime, stand still and count the skyscrapers. Manhattan has two hundred of them.

Stand still and stare in the store windows. Macy's is the biggest department store in the world. The toy store F. A. O. Schwarz has any toy you could wish for on its shelves.

Stand still beneath the nighttime lights that decorate Manhattan. The sign at Times Square spells out the news in twenty thousand flashing lights. Bright yellow taxicabs honk their way through the avenues like flocks of migrating geese.

At any hour, stand still and watch New York rush by. People are always hurrying to and from their jobs, selling or shopping, eating breakfast, lunch, or dinner. In New York, no one stands still for long. Soon *you'll* be going places and doing things, too.

Wherever you go in New York, getting there can be fun in itself, especially if you take the subway. Trains approach with a roar and a rattle and slide into the station with a squeal of brakes. Get a seat in the first car if you can, and watch the gleaming tracks unwinding in the darkness.

Of course, you can always hop a bus or hail a taxi. When the light on the cab's roof is lit, the taxi is available for you. If your destination's close enough, try walking instead. That's how Manhattan's first visitors got around.

MIDTOWN MANHATTAN

► See the Empire State Building, and see what you can see! There's an outdoor platform on the 86 floor, and the deck on the 102 floor has been compared to a glassed-in spaceship. Either observatory is a treat. Even on a cloudy day, it's fun to look down at the miniature cars and people below. On a clear day, you can see for fifty miles in all directions.

► Visit the United Nations and listen to the world! Since 1952, the United Nations Building has been the world's meeting house. Member nations try to solve problems from around the globe. Hear as well as watch the representatives through the special earphones that translate their words. Stop to mail a postcard before you leave. Since the U.N. is an international body, it issues its own postage stamps.

► Spend a whole afternoon at Rockefeller Center. Its nineteen skyscrapers cover twenty-two acres. The sunken plaza has outdoor ice skating in the winter, outdoor dining in the summer. If the weather's poor, duck down below. Wide walkways, lined with shops, join the buildings of Rockefeller Center together underground.

A. F. A. O. Schwarz is a paradise for children—and adults, as well. B. Macy's, the giant of department stores, covers an entire city block. C. News comes in a flash at Times Square. The square was named for a newspaper, *The New York Times*. D. Architects from thirteen countries cooperated to design the marble Secretariat Building for the United Nations.

OPPOSITE PAGE: A. Every weekday, hordes of commuters pass through magnificent Grand Central Terminal. B. At Rockefeller Center, Atlas holds up the world for all the world to see. C. Radio City Music Hall is the country's largest indoor theater. D. Remember to hail a taxi only when the light on the cab's roof is lit.

A. ►

B. ▼   C. ▼   D. ▼

A. ▲   B. ▼   C. ▼   D. ▼

▶ Applaud the show at Radio City Music Hall. It's right there at Rockefeller Center. The Music Hall's six thousand seats make it the largest theater in the United States. If you don't want to watch the stage show, take the backstage tour instead.

▶ Take in Times Square, the heart of the theater district. The Big Apple has more than thirty theaters, some with performances styled for kids. Times Square is a good place to find out what to see and where to go, for a visitor's information center is located there.

▶ Climb aboard the aircraft carrier *Intrepid*. This ship, active in both World War II and the Vietnam conflict, is now the *Intrepid* Sea-Air-Space Museum.

▶ Be amazed by a mall. Trump Tower looks like a pink marble palace, but it's really a vertical shopping mall!

▶ Remember MOMA. That's a museum, not a person. There are 150 museums in New York, so even if you visited one each day, it would take five months to see them all. The Museum of Modern Art is worth your time on any day. You'll find the best of modern painting and sculpture there.

UPTOWN MANHATTAN

▶ Boat, bike, skate (both roller and ice), ride (on a horse or in a carriage), jog, or stroll in Central Park. It's New York's playground, and anything you want to do is right there. Go to the Central Park Zoo, or see mechanical monkeys strike the bells on the Delacorte Musical Clock. Climb on the Alice in Wonderland statue, or be enchanted by the summertime Shakespeare-in-the-Park performances.

▶   Meet *Tyrannosaurus rex.* In the American Museum of Natural History, you'll see dinosaur skeletons galore. At the Naturemax, you'll gasp when nature comes alive on a motion picture screen four stories high and sixty-six feet wide! At the adjoining Hayden Planetarium, you'll gaze at stars and planets that are out of this world.

▶   Dress up in costumes at the Children's Museum of Manhattan.

▶   Make history come alive at the Museum of the City of New York. Everything from a Dutch fort to Victorian dollhouses are on display. "The Big Apple," a multimedia production, tells the New York story from 1624 until today.

▶   Don't miss the Met! The Metropolitan Museum of Art is the most famous in America, and you could spend your entire vacation in its fascinating galleries. Especially exciting is the Temple of Dendur, an original Egyptian temple from the banks of the Nile, reconstructed stone by stone in the Metropolitan.

▶   Tour Lincoln Center for the Performing Arts. This is home to music, drama, and dance. The center includes the Metropolitan Opera House, Avery Fisher Hall, the Juilliard School, and the New York State Theater. If you're lucky, you may find a rehearsal in progress in one of these buildings.

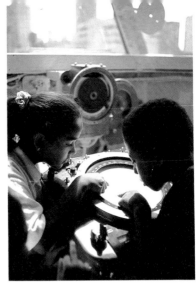

Although the aircraft carrier *Intrepid* is no longer on duty,
it sees plenty of action from tourists.

DOWNTOWN MANHATTAN

▶ Stroll through Greenwich Village, taking in the colorful shops. But watch out for the ghost of Edgar Allan Poe, who once lived there.

▶ Catch a boat bound for the Statue of Liberty on Liberty Island. Ferries leave seven days a week from Battery Park for this national monument. There, an elevator takes you to the top of the pedestal. But to reach Lady Liberty's crown, you'll have to climb a steep, twelve-story stairway.

▶ Sail past the Statue of Liberty on the Staten Island ferry. You'll get wonderful views, not only of Lady Liberty, but of Ellis Island, and of Governor's Island with its old fort. A ride on the Staten Island ferry is one of the best, shortest, and cheapest sea voyages.

▶ Don't pay a cent to visit the money center of the world: the New York Stock Exchange on Wall Street. Take a tour, or stand on the balcony and watch the scurrying below.

▶ Walk in the sky on the 110 floor of 2 World Trade Centers. Depending on the weather, you may really have your head in the clouds.

▶ See and sail at the South Street Seaport Museum. Board barques, schooners, and square-rigged sailing vessels on New York's "Street of Ships." In the summer, you can cruise about the harbor on the century-old two-masted ship, *Pioneer.* At any time of year, go to "The Seaport Experience," a show about the history of the area that puts you right in the middle of everything, even a storm at sea!

▶ Walk across the Brooklyn Bridge. There's a great view of Manhattan's skyline from beneath the bridge's spiderweb of steel girders.

BROOKLYN

▶ Discover the huge Brooklyn Museum, one of the finest anywhere. Its collections are outstanding, and only the museum in Cairo, Egypt, contains more mummies!

▶ Touch and find out in the Brooklyn Children's Museum. Founded in 1899, it's the world's oldest museum just for kids, and has hundreds of hands-on exhibits.

▶ Smile back at the white beluga whales at the New York Aquarium, located on Brooklyn's Coney Island. The whales swim and dive in a giant, one-hundred-thousand-gallon glass tank. The aquarium is home to seals and sharks, octopuses and penguins, and other sea creatures besides fish.

▶ Don't leave Coney Island without biting into one of Nathan's famous Coney Island hot dogs!

THE BRONX

▶ Watch and wonder at the Bronx Zoo, the largest collection of wild animals on earth. Riding one of the zoo's three trains adds to the fun. The Bengali Express, a monorail, takes you through Wild Asia. The Safari Train shows you Africa, as does the aerial tram, Skyfari.

▶ See New York as the Indians knew it. The New York Botanical Garden, located near the zoo, recreates the landscape that Henry Hudson saw.

QUEENS

▶   Visit the American Museum of the Moving Image, where 60,000 objects and exhibits from motion pictures and television dance before your eyes.

▶   See some historic sights, instead. The Bowne House and the Quaker Meeting House both date back to the days of the Dutch West India Company.

▶   Go to Flushing Meadows–Corona Park, where the Queens Museum, the Hall of Science, and the USTA National Tennis Center are among the attractions housed on the grounds of the 1964–65 New York World's Fair.

▶   Build a sandcastle at Rockaway Beach. Ten miles of sand stretch out for sunning and digging.

STATEN ISLAND

▶   Get off the Staten Island ferry when you get to Staten Island. Believe it or not, you'll see the highest coastal point between Maine and Florida: Todt Hill, 409 feet tall.

▶   Ride the bus to Snug Harbor Cultural Center. Once an old sailors' home, the center now houses art galleries, a music performance hall, and the Staten Island Children's Museum. The museum is fun for the whole family.

▶   Look into the past in the Richmond Restoration. This historic village features old houses, toys, dolls, and craftspeople demonstrating early-American skills.

▶   Go back to school at the Voorlezer's House. Dating back to 1695, it's the oldest elementary school in the U.S.

A.▲ B.▼ C.►

D.◄ E.▼

A. Don't miss the Brooklyn Children's Museum, B. the New York Aquarium, C. the Coney Island amusement park, D. Yankee Stadium (during baseball season), E. or the Bronx Zoo.

A POCKETFUL OF FACTS

NEW YORK STATE

On July 26, 1788, New York State joined the Union. Of the original thirteen American colonies, it was the eleventh state to be admitted. New York State was founded by the Dutch East India Company as the province of New Netherland.

New York ranks as the second largest state in population, after California. Measured in miles, it is the thirtieth state in size, and has sixty-two counties.

The capital of New York is Albany. The first capital was Kingston.

Mount Marcy in the Adirondack Mountains, 5,344 feet tall, is New York State's highest point. The lowest point is sea level.

New York State has more than eight thousand lakes, most of them carved out by glaciers during the Ice Age.

New York State is home to Niagara Falls on the Niagara River. These world-famous cascades include waterfalls that spill for 182 feet and splash two hundred thousand tons of water into the gorge every minute.

New York State is second only to California in manufacturing. New York is also known for its dairy products, and for its meat, fruits, and vegetables.

New York is the birthplace of four presidents of the United States: Martin Van Buren, Millard Fillmore, Theodore Roosevelt, and Franklin D. Roosevelt.

STATE SYMBOLS

State bird: Bluebird

State tree: Sugar maple

State animal: Beaver

State fish: Trout

State motto: *Excelsior!* (Latin for "Ever upward!")

State colors: Blue and orange

State nickname: The Empire State

State seal: The Hudson River with the sun, mountains, and
   two sailing ships. To the right stands Justice; to the left,
   Liberty; and above, a bald eagle on a globe.

State flag: The state seal on a dark blue field

NEW YORK CITY

New York City was founded by the Dutch in 1625 as New Amsterdam. It was incorporated as a city in 1653.

New York is the largest city in the United States, with a population of over seven and a quarter million people. It is the eighth largest city in the world.

New York City is made up of five boroughs: Manhattan, Bronx, Brooklyn, Queens, and Staten Island.

New York City is governed by a mayor and fifty-one council members, elected every four years.

New York City is number one in many ways. Its public school system is the largest in the world. The Port of New York handles the most cargo in the United States. The city has more parks and playgrounds and beaches than any other city in America. New York City has something for everyone, so it's sure to be number one on your list, too.

CITY SYMBOLS

The flag of the city of New York looks much like the flag that the Dutch West India company flew over New Amsterdam. The colors are the same: blue, white, and orange, which appear in three vertical stripes. The Dutch flag featured the company's initials in the center of the field, whereas the New York City flag shows the city seal.

The New York City seal pictures an American eagle, an English sailor, and a Manhattan Indian. It also shows the numerals 1664, the year England took the city from the Dutch.

For its song, the city has adopted "New York, New York."

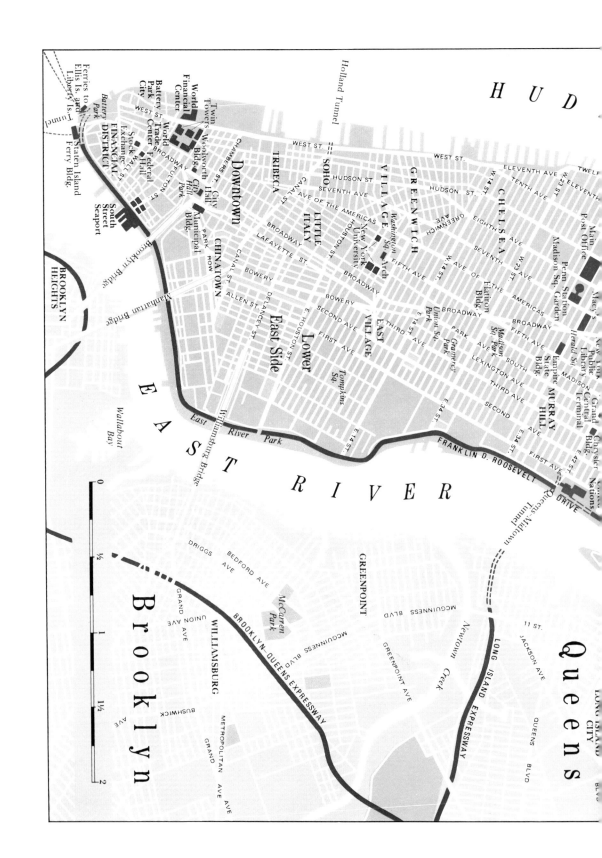

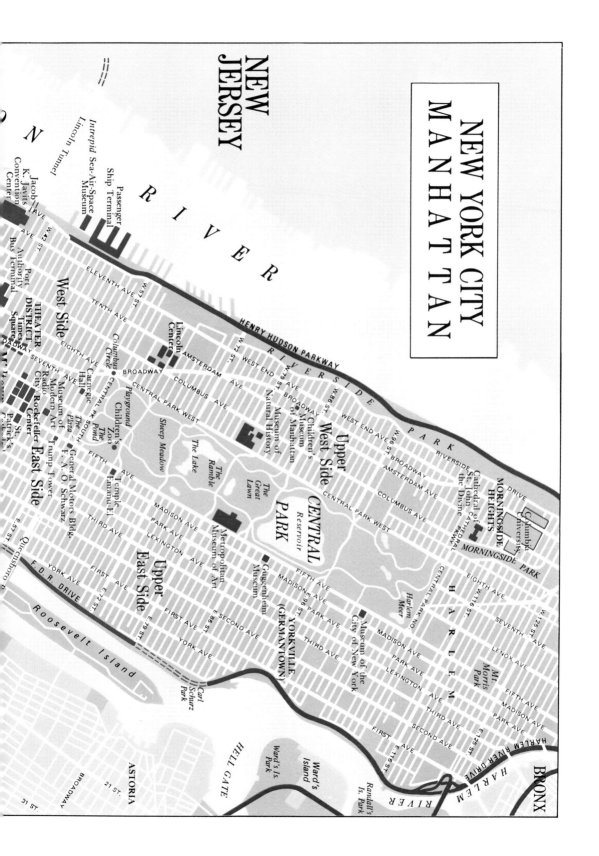

INDEX

←———→

Airports, 7
Algonquin Indians, 10, 16
Alice in Wonderland statue, 46
Astor, John Jacob, 24–26
Avery Fisher Hall, 47

Bartholdi, Frédéric A., 27
Battery Park, 49
Bengali Express, 50
Big Apple, 2, 38, 39, 47
Bowne House, 51
Bridges, 7, 27, 34, 50
Broadway, 26, 38
Bronx Zoo, 50
Brooklyn Bridge, 27, 34, 50
Brooklyn Museum, 50

Central Park, 6, 26, 38, 46–47
Central Park Zoo, 46
Champlain, Samuel de, 10, 16
Children's museums, 47, 50, 51
Chinatown, 35
Chrysler Building, 31
Coney Island, 50

Delacorte Musical Clock, 47
Duke of York, 14
Dutch East India Company, 9–10, 53
Dutch West India Company, 10, 55

Easter Parade, 6
East River, 3, 34
Ellis Island, 34–35, 49
Empire State, 20, 54
Empire State Building, 31, 43
Erie Canal, 22–23
Ethnic neighborhoods, 35

Federal Building, 19

Fifth Avenue, 6, 24, 26, 35
Fire, 13–14, 19, 23
Flatiron Building, 30
Flushing Meadows–Corona Park, 51
Fulton, Robert, 20

George III, 16–17
George Washington Bridge, 34
Gómez, Estéban, 9
Grand Central Terminal, 7
Greenwich Village, 35, 49

Hall of Science, 51
Harlem, 35
Harlem River, 3, 34
Hayden Planetarium, 47
High Bridge, 34
Housing, 11, 23–24, 38, 39
Hudson, Henry, 9–10
Hudson River, 2, 3, 10, 17, 20, 22, 34, 54

Immigrants, 11, 23, 34–35
Intrepid, aircraft carrier, 46

Janke, 15, 18
John F. Kennedy Airport, 7
Juilliard School, 47

La Guardia, Fiorello, 38
La Guardia Airport, 7
Liberty Island, 49
Lincoln Center for the Performing Arts, 47
Little India, 35
Little Italy, 35

Metropolitan Museum of Art, 26, 47
Metropolitan Opera House, 47

Monorail, 50
Mount Marcy, 53
Movies, 3, 51
Museums, 26, 46–47, 49–51

National Tennis Center, 51
Natural History Museum, 26, 47
Naturemax, 47
New Amsterdam, 10–14, 23, 54
New Netherland, 10, 14, 53
New Orange, 2, 14
New York Aquarium, 50
New York Bay, 2, 3, 9, 34
New York Botanical Garden, 50
New York State Theater, 47
New York Stock Exchange, 35, 49
New York World's Fair, 51
Niagara Falls, 53

Park Avenue, 35
Pennsylvania Station, 7
Pioneer, ship, 49
Police, 13–14, 24
Population, 6, 15, 20, 22, 27, 53, 54

Quaker Meeting House, 51
Queens Museum, 51

Radio City Music Hall, 46
Richmond Restoration, 51
Rockaway Beach, 51
Rockefeller Center, 6, 43, 46

Safari Train, 50
Saint Patrick's Cathedral, 26
Schwarz, F. A. O., 42
Ships, 20, 49

Skyfari, 50
Skyscrapers, 3, 30–31, 42
Snug Harbor Cultural Center, 51
Spanish Harlem, 35
Stamp Act, 16–17
Staten Island ferry, 6, 49, 51
Statue of Liberty, 7, 27, 49
Stock exchange, 35, 49
Stuyvesant, Peter, 13
Subway, 34, 42–43

Tammany Hall, 27, 38
Theaters, 38, 46
Times Square, 42, 46
Todt Hill, 51
Transportation, 31–34, 42–43
Triborough Bridge, 34
Trump Tower, 46

United Nations, 43

Verrazano, Giovanni da, 9
Verrazano-Narrows Bridge, 34
Voorlezer's House, 51

Wall Street, 13, 23, 35, 38
Wars, 15–19, 22, 24, 35, 38–39
Washington, George, 17–19, 20, 27, 38
Wollman Rink, 6
Woolworth Building, 30
World Trade Center, 31, 49

Yankees, 15, 18, 19

Zoos, 46, 50

A. At the Museum of Modern Art, you can even see a movie. B., C. In Central Park, penguins perform at the zoo, while mechanical animals perform at the Delacorte Musical Clock. D. At Lincoln Center, the New York State Theater is home to the New York City Ballet and the New York City Opera. E. And the Metropolitan Opera House presents some of the greatest opera and dance performances in the world.

A.▲   B.▼   C.▼

D.▼   E.▼